Lessons for TAR HEELS

written by **CAROLINE ROSEMARY** illustrated by **THOMAS HUSSUNG**

Copyright © 2021 by GreatestFan Publishing LLC

Text Copyright © 2021 by A.C. Gard

Illustrations Copyright © 2021 GreatestFan Publishing LLC

All Rights Reserved. No part of this book may be reproduced or published in any form or by any means, or stored in a database retrieval system, without the prior written permission of the Publisher.

Published by GreatestFan Publishing LLC, Chapel Hill, North Carolina

Book and cover design by Thomas Hussung

Printed and bound in China

Library of Congress Control Number: 2021917126
ISBN 978-0-9991453-3-3

10 9 8 7 6 5 4 3 2

To Carolina fans age 1 to 100

Put down the phone, and pick up a book.
Enjoy with a friend, cozy up in a nook.
Relive the past, and cheer for your team.
Learn lessons for life, and live out your dream.

www.lessonsfor.org

Caroline Rosemary

Favorite Song:
Carolina in My Mind

Favorite Color:
Carolina Blue

Favorite Food:
Brunch at The Carolina Inn

Favorite Tar Heels in History:
Mia Hamm
Dré Bly
Roy Williams

Favorite Carolina Moment:
Any time Carolina beats Duke

Author's Pet:
Baby ram named Dean

We start this little story, in the Old North State,
A nice place to call home, completely first rate.
Where people are nice, they stop to say "Hi!"
And they'll give you a wave, as they drive on by.

A magical place, where there's plenty to do,
From mountains to sea, there is something for you.

In the sand on a beach, in the summer we'll play,
Having fun in the woods, in blue skies or gray.

On top of a hill, a village we know,
A quaint college town, great minds learn and grow.
Big dreams, smart kids, they'll conquer it all,
Big problems to solve, they'll answer the call.

Flowers bloom, leaves turn, we sing Hark The Sound,
Brick path under foot, stone walls all around.
Good luck will be yours, when you sip from the Well,
A smile on your face, at the sound of the bell.

Spend time in the Pit, on a perfect fall day,
Stroll slow through the Quad, where kids often play.
No doubt you'll enjoy, with that smile on your face,
And soon fall in love, with this wonderful place.

So many folks, have called this place home,
Always to return, wherever they roam.
Some great with their feet, some hang in the air,
With talent and grace, no one can compare.

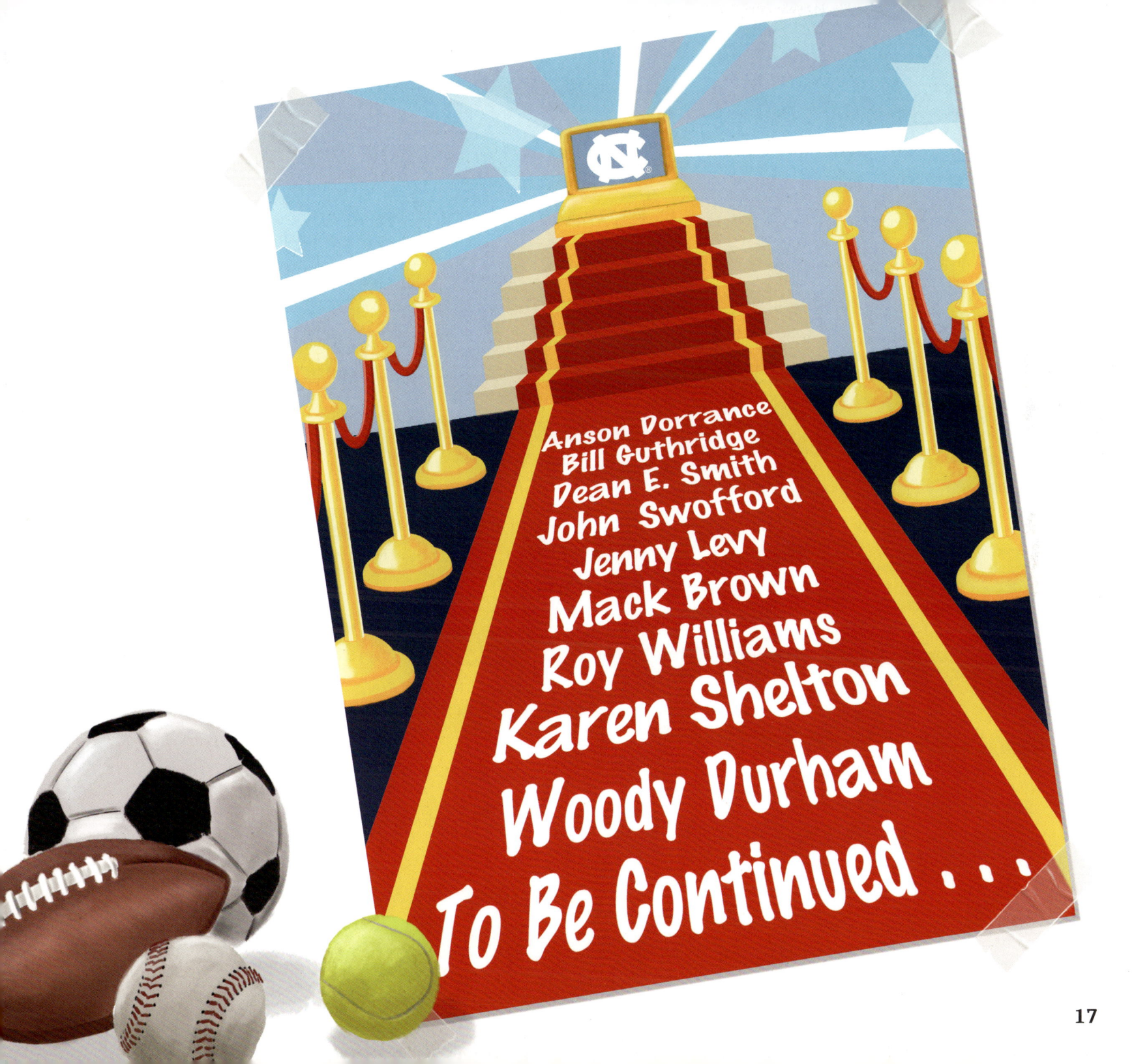

MJ, LT, Mia, Tyler and Vince.
They all walked the grounds, wasn't hard to convince.
Whether player or coach, Tar Heels seize the day.
You name the sport, and we'll show up to play.

Now these folks are nice, and they make us all proud,
They hold their heads high, stand out in a crowd.
But what can we learn, from others so great?
Can we be like them, or is it just fate?

Now listen real close, and lend me your ear.
A little closer, lean in, this is something to hear.
Whatever you dream, you can make it come true.
It's no secret you see, here's just what to do.

First make up your bed, when the sun wakes you up.
Put a smile on your face, give some rubs to your pup.
Do chores, eat your greens, say your prayers every day.
Keep that smile all day long, in blue skies or gray.

Try your best at all things, no matter what you may do,
In school, at your craft, and your favorite sports too.

Favorite Sports:
Baseball
Basketball
Cross Country
Fencing
Field Hockey
Football
Golf
Gymnastics
Lacrosse
Quidditch
Rowing
Sailing
Soccer
Softball
Swimming + Diving
Tennis
Track + Field
Ultimate Frisbee
Water Polo
Wrestling

Be a good friend to all, from the east and the west,
Welcome all with a smile, put them all to the test.

Get the basics down pat, be part of a team,
Always shoot for the stars, and remember your dream.
Work hard and compete, do your best, nothing more,
And remember the journey, far more than the score.

Know much more important, than the skills of the sport,
Are the lessons you learn, that you'll take from the court.

Show respect for others, give thanks for the pass.
Always play together, pay attention in class.

Dress nice, walk tall, keep a smile on your face.
Focus not on the prize, but the fun of the chase.
Please do your best, though you can't always win.
Be kind to all, no matter color of skin.

And as you grow up, keep your fire for the game.
Stay a child in your heart, don't extinguish the flame.
Cheer loud for your team, but respect those you play.
'Cause we all can be friends, at the end of the day.

So when you're on top, where you'll certainly be,
Take a good look around, like a bird in a tree.

See family and friends, those who helped on the way.
Lending hands to support, never matter the day.

And when you're in town, stop by and check in.
Wear your colors with pride, check to see how we've been.
You're a Tar Heel for life, blue and white head to toe.
Thanks for sharing your time, now Go Tar Heels Go!

The End

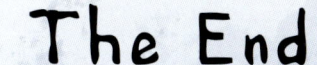

Did You Know ... ?

We encourage children and adults to put down their phones and pick up a book.

Excessive screen time has a negative impact on children's brain development, concentration, socialization and ability to build a large vocabulary. Children learn through relationships and back-and-forth interactions, including the interactions that occur when reading with others. Reading with others can also help with problem behaviors like hyperactivity, aggression and attention issues.

Playing sports and being a fan can also positively impact childhood development. In addition to physical and mental health benefits, playing sports can improve self-esteem, improve grades and help children develop better social skills.

Through sports, we can all learn virtues such as fairness, cooperation and respect for rules. Fandom provides a built-in community and can boost one's sense of well-being. Identifying with a favorite team can improve emotional, psychological and social health.

Support UNC Athletics
https://ramsclub.com/

p.7
The Old North State is a nickname for the state of North Carolina and the official state song, written by William Gaston in 1835.

p.7
Chapel Hill is located in central North Carolina, and is the home of the University of North Carolina at Chapel Hill ("UNC"). Chapel Hill was founded in 1789, and along with neighboring cities Durham and Raleigh, make up the Research Triangle.

p.11
Chartered in 1789, UNC is a public research university and the nation's first public university.

p.12
Hark The Sound is UNC's alma mater, written by William Starr Myers (class of 1897). Hark The Sound is sung following all sporting events on campus, typically followed by the University's fight song, I'm a Tar Heel Born.

p.12
South Building was one of the first buildings built on campus, construction beginning around 1798. It currently houses the Office of the Chancellor. South Building is located in the heart of campus across the street from the Old Well.

p.12
The Old Well, perhaps the most recognized symbol of the University, is located on campus at the southern end of McCorkle Place.

p.12
The Morehead-Patterson Bell Tower ("Bell Tower") was completed in 1931.

p.15
The Pit is the nickname of the popular courtyard next to the Carolina Union on main campus.

p.15
The Quad refers to the Upper or Lower Quad that make up central campus. Quad is an abbreviation for quadrangle, which is a space or courtyard, often square or rectangular in shape, typically surrounded by buildings.

p.17
Anson Dorrance (b. 1951) is the head coach of the UNC Women's Soccer Team and has coached UNC to 22 women's soccer National Championships and counting. Dorrance is a member of the National Soccer Hall of Fame.

p.17
Bill Guthridge (1937 - 2015) was an assistant UNC Men's Basketball coach to Dean Smith for thirty years, helping guide UNC to two NCAA Championships. Guthridge is a member of the Assistant Coaches Hall of Fame. Guthridge was UNC Men's Basketball head coach from 1997 to 2000.

p.17
Dean E. Smith (1931 - 2015) was the head coach of the UNC Men's Basketball Team from 1961 to 1997 and coached UNC to NCAA Championships in 1982 and 1993. He is a member of the Naismith Memorial Basketball Hall of Fame and received the Presidential Medal of Freedom for both his excellence in coaching and his fight for civil rights.

p.17
John Swofford (b. 1948) was a Morehead-Cain scholar at UNC and played on the football team from 1970 to 1971. He was the Athletic Director at UNC from 1980 to 1997 and the Atlantic Coast Conference Commissioner from 1997 to 2021.

p.17
Jenny Levy (b. 1969) has been the head coach of the UNC Women's Lacrosse Team for over 25 years and coached UNC to NCAA Championships in 2013 and 2016. She is one of the most successful coaches in women's lacrosse history and a member of the National Lacrosse Hall of Fame.

p.17
Mack Brown (b. 1951) was the head coach of the UNC football team from 1988 to 1997, and was hired back as the head coach at UNC in 2019. Brown is a member of the College Football Hall of Fame and won the BCS National Championship in 2005 as head coach at the University of Texas.

p.17
Roy Williams (b. 1950) was an assistant coach for the UNC Men's Basketball Team from 1978 to 1988 under Dean Smith before serving as the Kansas Jayhawks head coach from 1988 to 2003.
Williams returned to UNC in 2003 as the head Men's Basketball coach and led UNC to NCAA Championships in 2005, 2009 and 2017. Williams is a member of the Naismith Memorial Basketball Hall of Fame.

p.17
Karen Shelton (b. 1957) is the head coach of the UNC Women's Field Hockey Team and the winningest field hockey coach in NCAA history. Shelton has coached UNC to 9 NCAA championships and counting. Shelton is a member of the National Field Hockey Coaches Association Hall of Fame and the USA Field Hockey Hall of Fame.

p.17
Woody Durham (1941 - 2018) was the play-by-play radio announcer for UNC Men's Basketball and Football from 1971 to 2011 and is a member of the National Sports Media Association Hall of Fame.

p.18
Michael Jordan (b. 1963) (aka "MJ" and "Air Jordan") played shooting guard for the UNC Men's Basketball Team from 1981 to 1984, and then professionally in the NBA for the Chicago Bulls and Washington Wizards. Jordan is considered the greatest basketball player of all time, earning him the nickname the G.O.A.T. (Greatest Of All Time). Jordan is a member of the Naismith Memorial Basketball Hall of Fame and received the Presidential Medal of Freedom.

p.18
Lawrence Taylor (b. 1959) (aka "LT") played defense for the UNC Football Team from 1978 to 1981, and then professionally in the NFL for the New York Giants. Taylor is considered the greatest defensive football player of all time. Taylor is a member of the Pro Football Hall of Fame.

p.18
Mia Hamm (b. 1972) played forward for the UNC Women's Soccer Team from 1989 to 1993, for the United States Women's National Team from 1987 to 2005 and professionally for the Washington Freedom from 2001 to 2003. Hamm is considered one of the greatest women's soccer players of all time and is a member of the National Soccer Hall of Fame.

p.18
Tyler Hansbrough (b. 1985) (aka "Psycho T") played power forward/center for the UNC Men's Basketball Team from 2005 to 2009 and then professionally. Hansbrough lead UNC to the 2009 NCAA Championship.

p.18
Vince Carter (b. 1977) (aka "Vinsanity" and "Half Man Half Amazing") played shooting guard for the UNC Men's Basketball Team from 1995 to 1998, and then professionally in the NBA from 1998 to 2020.

www.lessonsfor.org